A DAPPLED PATH

by
Gai-Louise Partridge

For Little Mummy Bear

{who made me promise to publish before she dies}

For Little Mummy Bear

who made me promise to publish before she goes

<u>*"Note to the Reader"*</u>

Content warning:

This publication contains material which
some readers may find confronting.

If affected, I implore you to please reach out to your preferred
support or consult the list of support resources listed in the
back of this book for a service that will suit your needs.

First published 2023 by Partridges in Print, Aust. via Lulu Press, Inc.

2nd print October 2023

12345678910

A catalogue record for this book is available from the National Library of Australia

NATIONAL LIBRARY OF AUSTRALIA

ISBN: 978-0-9873660-0-9

Cover and text: GL Partridge
Cover image: Jo Morgan
Printed by: Lulu Press, Inc.

I acknowledge the Traditional Custodians of the lands on which this body of work was created, this lands first storytellers. I honour Aboriginal and Torres Strait Islander peoples' continuous connection to Country, waters, skies, and communities. I celebrate Aboriginal and Torres Strait Islander stories, traditions, and living cultures; and pay my respects to Elders past, present, and emerging.

Table of Contents

Table of Contents – continued

A Dappled Path

The following is an anthology of poems, stories, and notations that meander along the path of life. Ever-changing shades of light and dark within the landscape of love and torment, laughter and tears, and clawing a way back out of that deep, fetid well of despair.

Why this book? Well, I have a habit of working through my feelings on paper. Sometimes the only way back from the edge, for me, is to let the tide of emotion (or lack thereof) out before it consumes me. I have occasionally found myself hanging, rather precariously, and with a failing grip, to no more than a straggly root exposed on the crumbling cliff face of self-destruction. You will see those moments within these pages. You will also see my defiant triumph over the enfolding darkness, to embrace life once again in all its crazy glory.

Life can be a wonderful experience if we can just push through to find the beauty in it again. We know that not everyone makes it back, so it is my hope this book can show that there IS a path. It may not be possible to shake that Black Dog completely. Perhaps, with a little work, we could train it to walk to heel with compassion and patience...   and treats.

Well, that, and I promised my mother!

It was always the plan for my sister to provide sketches and small artworks to accompany the works within. We were both looking forward to the collaboration. I have been her most ardent fan, from the day she put her high-school art submission behind our bedroom door. I have no idea how old I was, but she had left home before I'd turned seven.

I was looking forward to her (literally) drawing out the beauty trapped within the heartache of my words and expanding on the vibrant glimpses. I will never know how she would have reinterpreted my words, as she left us mere mortals to take up her post in the Seelie Court at Tatiana's side some years ago. In her honour, I have included as many of my favourite pieces as I could respectfully squeeze in, with deepest gratitude to her family and estate.

Dear reader, I invite you to join me on the journey....

1

Happy and Bright

Poppet

Poppet, though you left our care, you never left our hearts.
We loved you then and still do now, even though we are apart.
When thinking back on times with you, we always crack a smile.
We'd love to sit and talk with you and reminisce a while.

Remember when we used to ask, "Are you in that bathtub yet?"
And you'd say "Yes!" but funny how you were not even wet.
You knew you shouldn't tell a fib, so you'd jump in, clothes and all,
But 'forget' to turn the water on. At least you never got a scald.

Oh, how we miss your smiling face, your funny little ways.
We miss you more and more and <u>more</u> each and every passing day,
So, if, by chance, you'd like to see your aunties and Jinxi,
We'd be so happy, we'd jump for joy, we'd even dance with glee!

We loved you then, we love you now. I'll say it once again.
We tried to do our best for you but failed you back then.
We know you're in a better home. We have no doubt of that,
But we'd like to share some happy times with you, and that's a fact.

So, if you can, we'd like to ask,
Please forgive mistakes we made,
And remember once more there were times,
We danced and sang and played.

Mine by Heart

From the moment a mother knows a child grows within,
They say that a bond forms, webs of love start to spin.

Those moments with you I was not meant to share,
But there's no denying the bond that is there.

The love that I hold in my heart just for you,
Can never be taken or broken in two.

Though born to another I consider you Daughter,
And I'll always be there, just like a Mum oughta.

23rd February 2011

<u>Caspa</u>

With the hardest years at your feet,
I watch you smile and laugh.
Am I a fool to believe,
There are no demons in your past.

Haunted dreams in which you cried.
Could it be my instincts lied?
I pray to every god I know,
That it was just some freaky show.

Caspa, e'er my friendly ghost,
Keep your head held high.
What I want for you the most,
Is that you learn to fly.

2001

Saint Pudi the Patient

You do it for love, not for the praise,
But if you were paid, you'd be due for a raise.
Your efforts are tireless, or seemingly so,
And for thanks you are left wondering,
Will she stay? Will she go?

It's not hard to see all the good work you do.
If the church needs a saint, look no further than you.
Without complaint you give away,
Thoughts of your own needs, day after day.

You may say it's nothing, not a great sacrifice,
But her care has come at a fairly large price.
Your life at a halt, no time of your own.
Just a friend to pop over, a voice on the phone.

What keeps you going when you just want to scream?
Will you wake up one day to find it all was a dream?
No, you really have taken one day at a time,
To let this girl heal, so her life will be fine.

Don't bow your head and say it's the least.
We can see she's an angel, but often a beast,
And still, you continue to give loving care,
When it seems that her parents, no burden will share.

Now hold high your head for it's never a sin,
To show the whole world how God looks from within,
For in you I can see what they all try to teach,
That there is a true god, a god you can reach.

26th June 2006

For David*

Though his essence has rejoined his maker,
And his body is needed no more,
He leaves behind his laughter and love,
To even up the score.

For these gifts can never be taken.
Once given, they e'er remain,
Until, in some distant future,
Souls are united again.

*And later adapted for use by many others.

What Colour is a Red Rose?

When asked the colour of a red rose,
One might answer 'Red, I suppose,'
But look again and you might see,
The colours which appear to me.

Red of petal, green of stem.
The same of leaf and even then,
The colours that dance within that rose,
Are more abundant than all of those.

How many reds appear to you,
And shades of green and white and blue?
Are you surprised that I said blue?
That's not the only hidden hue.

When next you see a rose of red,
Think twice before you turn your head.
That humble rose of red you're seeing,
Holds a rainbow within its being.

1994

21

Seelie Court of the Magic Coral Tree

Underneath the coral tree,
Magic came to life.
The fairy kings and queens with,
Their territories in strife.

Bright red robes of finery,
With little golden crowns.
It mattered not to me they were,
Merely petals fallen down.

I'd bravely go to war and,
Defend against the army.
Oh, what fun I had when,
The sun was warm and balmy.

My mother in her summer dress,
Watching me at play.
Underneath the coral tree.
Oh, what a perfect day.

24th September 2023 12:45

2

<u>Dark(ish)</u>

Safe Within My Bubble

Just a few years ago I was alone,
But I healed every week.
My life was going so well,
And I was happy.
Then I thought of myself,
And life took a downward turn.

I find myself with similar,
Circumstances now.
I am alone again.
The need to heal is strong,
But I need to find a safe place,
In which to give all I am able.

I feel the pull but can't find the direction.

13th September 2001

The Game

Trembling fingers reached out to touch the vision of beauty before her, but they met only the inky darkness of an empty night. Regardless, the love that lay just below the surface once again swelled and threatened to engulf her. She fought with all her might, but in vain. The love rose from within, first glowing then so blinding bright and warm and intense… and as always, with it came the pain. Love so pure no human being could endure it. With a scream she became one with the love and the last she knew she was scattered to the night sky in a billion tiny pieces, not unlike a starburst of fireworks.

Love…. It is a dark and dangerous game….

One you cannot play to win.

31st July 2001 01:47

You Were There

Tears to wash away the pain.
Tears to wash away the shame.
So many tears,
For so many years.
Will there ever be peace again?

Reach out to take you in my arms.
Reach out to hide away from harm.
But you were there,
And didn't care.
I'm left with a tarnished lucky charm.

2001

Dr Sam

"The saddest aspect of my life to date…,"
Is how long I've lived with self-loathing and hate.
It's not about love and what others have done,
It's about me not seeing <u>I'm</u> the important one.

It's easy to write this and make it sound bright,
When I've only just seen you at seven tonight.
I'm curious to see if my mood gains momentum,
Or whether I revert to my usual doldrum.

Once Too Personal to Publish.

I'm a foreigner in my own life.
Don't know the language,
Don't understand the customs.
Stumbling blindly through,
Never really knowing.

3

Darker

A Scar For Life

You can wipe the blood from the wall.
The bruises, they will fade.
A torn dress can be mended,
But the heart is scarred forever.

The stitches come out next week.
I bought a new set of glasses today.
The glue has dried on the table,
But my heart is scarred forever.

We're laughing together again.
The love is so intense.
You touch my skin so gently,
But this heart is scarred forever.

The boxes are scattered all over the floor.
I've unpacked the CD's, the records, and books.
I fall into bed and silently miss you,
And this heart is scarred forever.

Inspired by Cassie's note:
"Blood dries, wounds heal, but a broken heart is a scar for life."

18th August 2001

I write of death and calm enfolds me,
In its safe and warm embrace.
I think of death and peace takes me,
To a quiet perfect place.

I write of love and cold corrupts me.
The pain upon my face.
To think of love is tantamount,
To torture and disgrace.

30th October 2012

13.09.2001

Time slows as the windows behind me shatter. I don't know it yet, but I have less than a second to live. I turn to see what caused the glass to break and it takes me a moment to register that I am looking at the nose of a plane, hurtling toward me. I don't quite have time to finish wondering WHY there's a plane in my office, nor do I have time to run before the life I knew is eliminated.

I DO have time however, to realise I forgot to take the meat out of the freezer this morning. Jan had called out from the kids' room, and I didn't do it. I forgot. I was going to do it when I took my cup to the sink.

I had time, too, to make a list of all the things I'll never do again, like hold my wife and tell her that I love her – I should have done that more often. Or ruffle Jason's hair as he shows me his latest 'work of art.' He's four and blonde as blonde, though both my wife and I are dark. I have time to think of the fun we've had teasing each other over that. Matty, the elder boy, is as dark as us. Both the kids look so much like me that there's no worries about that, but I'll miss the banter. I won't be walking the dog anymore.

Oh hell!! Jan's birthday present is on lay away and no-one knows about it! I went into so much detail with the designer because I wanted her to take one look at it and know that she is my everything. That in the hustle and bustle of the mundane, I love her more than life itself. That my love hasn't faded over time but grown deeper. How will she know that now? I should have just told her. Every day.

I'm still thinking these thoughts when I realise, I'm no longer looking at the nose of a plane tearing up the office. I don't really know where I am. There is no sound, no light, no anything. I can't feel anything. Did I miss my final moment? How weird. But if that's the case, where am I now?

I need to stop and think back. I was so distracted thinking of all the other stuff. I go back over everything and try to remember anything since I was confronted by that stark reality of impending utter destruction, but there is nothing after that moment. Just my thoughts. Clearly, I can't be dead, or I wouldn't still be thinking rationally, right? Maybe I'm just trapped, and it's dark because there obviously isn't any electricity. It's the only answer my mind will accept and I'm certain someone will come to help soon.

I think of my shoes and realise they are probably ruined now. What a waste. So brand new that I'm still breaking them in. I wish I hadn't fought with Jan over the cost now. It had seemed so important, at the time, that I have high quality shoes. You know that saying about the cut of a man's suit? A good suit without the shoes to go with it are a rookie error that is so easy to spot. It's not just the quality of your work that gets you ahead, in this town. To be successful, you need to look successful. I know the whole family could have had new shoes all year for the price of this one pair and it suddenly doesn't seem so important. I just hope I make it back home to them so I ca...

Shouldn't I be hurting? I should feel pain or something. I should be able to hear something. Why can't I hear anything? Where IS everyone?

I CAN'T FEEL ANYTHING!

WHERE AM I?!!

SOMEBODY?!

…ANYBODY!!!

Heaven

Open wide your slender legs,
And let the games begin.
You'd let the whole world come inside,
But never let them in.

If they only understood you.
If you only knew yourself,
That your body's there for anyone,
But your soul's up on the shelf.

It never sees the light of day,
Not since you were a kid.
Heaven help you if you dust it off,
It'll put your whole life in a skid.

Just go away, I don't need to see,
Your trail of broken hearts,
While mine remains together,
In its many jagged parts.

17th August 2001

A Brief Reprieve

Don't give in, don't let them win.
Keep your posture, raise your chin.
Instead of loss, think fairy floss.
Remind yourself, 'You've got this, Boss.'

At every turn, there'll be some worm,
Who wants to cause undue concern.
Without disgrace each trial you face,
Will put your doubters in their place.

Brave self-talk until you baulk.
You should have turned and made them walk.
Up you hop and show that lot,
When backed up tight you'll come out hot.

If it were me, I'd surely flee.
I'm nowhere near as brave as thee.

04:00

Driving all day to no particular destination.
I get there and come on back again.
Turn around and choose a new direction.
Tell myself it's all about the journey.

Enjoy the scenery and tell tales of exploration.
Never admit to anyone, the tank's on empty.
Come and go, spontaneous inspiration.
No such thing as lost, only scenic routes.

How long can you maintain the illusion?
You'll take a bend too fast, one day.
Become an overnight crashing sensation.
As long as no one knows the truth.

So much for your imagination.
Change the CD, sing a whole new tune,
And make believe in restoration,
Whilst the wheels keep turning.

Make your newest resolution.
Turn the car around.
Headlights, your eternal illumination,
As you finally arrive home.

The crumbling cliffs echo your elation.
Waves crash against its base in welcome.
Flames burst forth from the eruption,
As a front wheel spins in fond farewell.

17th August 2001

<u>4</u>

<u>Darkest</u>

A Conversation with Oblivion

So, you think you've done well.
Made it through another night.
As long as you remember,
You haven't won this fight.

I'll be back before you know it,
Or maybe I will wait.
Just keep on smiling, baby,
'Til I bring you to your fate.

It might not be today,
Tonight, or even next week,
But just keep one eye open.
I'll be back under guise of sleep.

If you'd just let me go, you could have me all to yourself. I don't want to be here, any more than you WANT me here. I don't know how to leave so come back any time and if you come back with answers, I'll greet you with open arms.

Oh, for the bliss of dark oblivion. You threaten but if you only knew how I desire you. Above no other, you stand alone as the one thing that I crave most with all that I am.

10th September 2001   22:00

Tenuous

Where can I go to shut out the sound?
I smile for a moment then my heart starts to pound.
The shuffles of feet on putrid stone floors.
The sound as their fingers claw at the doors.

Was feeling so good 'til I read what I wrote.
My strength floats away on a single dust mote.
I'll be okay, but it just goes to prove,
That my positive outlook's so easy to lose.

Darkeness in Darkness

Darkeness, open your arms,
I long for your embrace.
I am lonely without you,
Only you can love this face.

Kiss away this pain,
Kiss away this shame.
Take this soul and,
Cleanse it with your flame.

Dance with me cheek to cheek,
Waltz me 'round the room.
Hold me as a lover would,
While we hum our private tune.

I won't look back,
If you take me away from here.
I can leave now if you're ready,
Now the way is clear.

31st July 2001 01:30

5

From the Bottom of the Well

Wel[come] [t]o the world of GL. That worthless speck of dust [...] is eve[r] [n]othing more than so much canine faecal matter th[at you] ste[...]d in one day, on your way to something truly impor[tant]. She [w]hose only purpose in life is to lay before you hum[bly] beg[...]g that you spit upon her, blessed in your filth. Visit thi[...] and [...]ow true disgust. Explore the unchartered depths of h[er] [...] exi[ste]nce so you can fully appreciate the worthlessness of [this] ins[ign]ificant, pathetic excuse for a soul. Never before has t[here] be[en] [s]uch a blatant waste of human tissue. Watch as she w[...] in [...] sewer of her life's mistakes and drinks deeply of its slimy [...] [conten]ts, believing that she tastes instead life's nectar of be[auty] and [w]onder. Watch her strive to dream, never realising th[at she] [...] [b]uilds those castles of crystal with the scum from the [walls] of [this] squalid dungeon. Laugh with us all as she believes [...] tha[t] [...]ending her world and finding a new life full of love [and] pas[...], when in fact she lays thrashing in her own waste, [...] and [h]owling like the hell-beast she is. This is no human, no c[...] of [...] [a]nd beauty. This is life's most foul miscreation. Kill it [...] is n[o] [p]lace in this world for one so twisted, deformed, and [...] The [s]tench of its existence cannot hope to be eliminated whilst [it] live[s]. [TH]E FOUL BEAST. You are not welcome here. You are ban[ished] from [th]is place. You are nothing & this world turns its back o[n you] [no]t just for now bu[...] A[L]WAYS AND FOREVER!!

You're shocked the cause of my dysfunction,
Within these pages had no mention.
Isn't that too much for this wee book?
There is no art in what he took.

The horror trapped within my soul,
Would send me right back down that hole,
If I should let it from its cage,
My default setting is death or rage.

Stolen dreams when childhood games,
Ended up always the same.
We'll never know what I'd have been,
Without the torture down between.

Would I have set the world afire?
Upon the stage, Streetcar Desire?
But on my forehead glowed his stamp,
I was just his well-trained tramp.

Passed around to earn him friends.
Poked and prodded for measurements.
Ladybirds I sought to save,
The evil deeds that I forgave.

They said I'd heal best once I did.
They lied. I'm daily in a skid.
By sheer willpower I hold on tight.
No wonder I have no more fight.

So please don't ask why I don't write,
Of how that vile creep changed my life.

6

Broken Hearts and Healing Parts

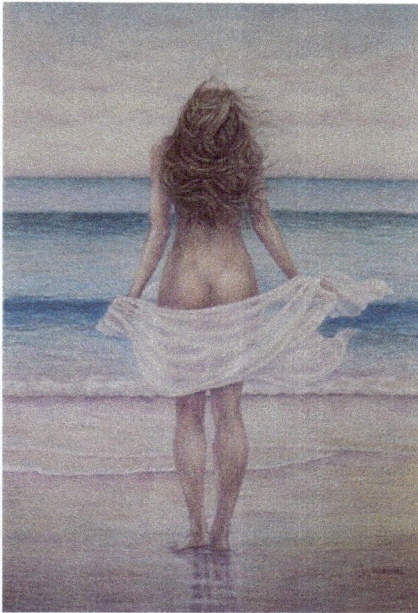

I don't wanna talk 'bout last days anymore,
I'm so sick of being a suicide whore.
It's not gonna happen, obviously,
Or I wouldn't be here now writing of me.

Let's talk about presents and what to give who,
And what else is so great that I really must do.
CD racks to buy and collections to sort, ☺
And nights by the fire, sipping on port.

Let's make a list of the things that I'd buy,
And where I should go if I only would fly.
Nothing outrageous that's so out of reach,
Just life simple pleasure's, a walk on the beach.

Let's banish my demons, start healing my soul,
So I can forgive and discover my role.
I need to discover just who I am,
I need you to help me get outta this sham.

No more stone dungeons, walls covered in slime,
With fingers left bleeding where I've tried to climb.
No more dark sewers with screams behind doors,
And faces like mirrors with festering sores.

Just one goal a week to begin life anew,
Before long one achievement becomes quite a few.
It can't be too hard to find a reason to live,
Hey, maybe it's me I need to forgive.

Love well

I wish you love and happiness.
It doesn't make me love you less,
And even though you left a hole,
That festered down into my soul,
I will find a way to heal,
And even, one day, maybe feel.

There is enough of me left to care,
That life is always better shared,
So, go, my friend. I mean no harm.
Find comfort in another's arms.

And once again I'll close this book,
On the detour which my life was took.

Your eyes were brown,
Like sweet warm chocolate.
Your skin so soft,
Like silk or velvet.

But that was so very long ago.
A lot has changed since then.
It hurts so much to look back,
To our time together when,

"I love you" seemed like the truth,
But who was kidding who?
No matter how far back I go,
Before we started, we were through.

I'm glad you live without regret.
It means you can never be sad,
But for me it's harder to forget,
All we had that made me glad.

5th September 2001 23:35

Kemba

Someone's playing songs that remind me of you.
I did it all so wrong, can't believe that we're through.
Yes, you were cruel with the things that you did.
Why'd I make that stupid rule?
Why didn't I forgive?

So many others did the same.
I forgave them every time.
When it came to you, I said "Never again,"
But without you, nothings fine.

I tried to love somebody else,
But you're with me everywhere,
And even though I'm by myself,
I just can't seem to care.
I'd rather live my life alone,
Than share a heart that's yours.
Maybe in time I can atone,
For all my many flaws.

No one before and no one since
Could make me feel this good…

Oh, who was I trying to convince?

18th – 19th August 2001

5:30

I need a new song.
None of the old ones make me want to dance.
I need a new song.
One to make me want to take another chance.

I need a new song
To break me out of this trance.
I need a new song.
I need a new romance.

What's your name anyway?
How do I introduce you?
Wanna take the whole day.
I'd like to get to know you.

We've all been through the pain.
It's something we all understand,
But if you're willing to try again,
Just take me by the hand.

Leave the past behind us.
We've conquered nights dark sky.
All I ask is a little trust,
So baby, we can fly.

17th August 2001

59

On Reflection

Not every decision I've made was good,
Not every choice was right.
But I made it here, despite myself and,
I'm happy enough tonight.

I've driven fast, toward a cliff,
In a front-wheel drive.
A risen mound in thick, tall grass,
Is why I'm here alive.

The magic number paracetamol,
I've chewed and swallowed down,
And woke up in the morning,
So got dressed 'cause work would frown.

I've researched how to end my life,
In many countless ways,
Yet here I am. I have survived,
To see those better days.

Azaleas are blooming, now.
In purple, peach and pink.
My cat is purring on my lap.
Life's a blessing now, I think.

There's music on the stereo.
I've a coffee at my side.
The years of feeling all and nothing
Were really quite the ride.

24th September 2023 00:00

7

For Mum

Mother's Love

A lifetime of love I've had from you,
Though I gave you so much pain.
From labour through my teenage years,
Then beyond that, and again.

And yet I know, despite your years,
I could call on you, in need,
So how can I repay that faith,
With a similar act or deed?

There is no way that I can see,
To express my love for you,
Other than, perhaps or not,
Honour MYSELF as you would do.

For if I am worthy of your love,
Unconditional and without end,
It stands to reason I must also be,
My own, most beloved friend.

A Teen Grows Up

We've had our fair share of clashes,
Had opposing points of view,
But I am the woman I am today,
Largely because of you.

You've taught me to be proud and strong.
To admit when I am wrong,
To live my life with honesty,
And know where I belong.

10th September 2001   8.50pm

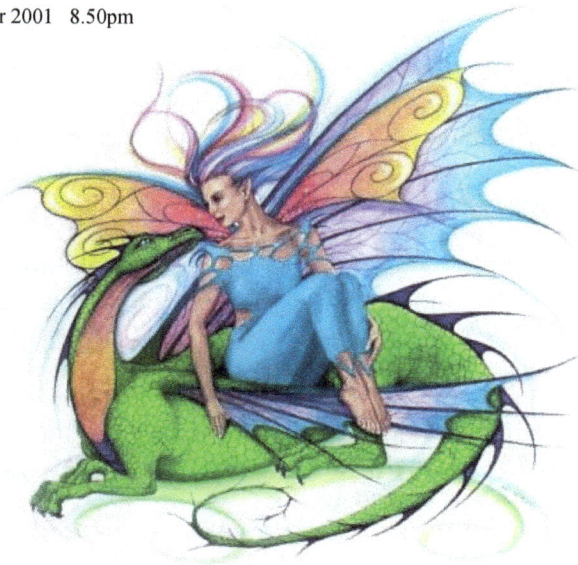

Happiest 90th birthday and wake,

Little Mummy Bear.

You, my littlest Mummy Bear,
Are something to behold.
From harsh beginnings who'd have thought,
You'd ever get this old.
From tales of orphanage days bygone.
The stories I've been told.
You must have prayed for their fiery hell,
Just to stop from being cold.

When I think of things you've taught me,
It's compassion, love, and strength.
Integrity and honesty you've coached me in at length.
I look at you and I can see such character in depth.
I'll succeed while ever I can share in just one tiny tenth.

You wanted to hear what I would say,
When your time was past.
I know there's one or two out there who really were aghast.
I think it's simply fabulous you're around to hear, at last.
That 90 years isn't long enough, so don't go anywhere fast.

We still have many cards to make, and cushions left to sew.
We've stories waiting to be shared of things I didn't know.
We've lots of laughs still undiscovered,
With nowhere else to go,
But spilling out at yet another tale of hilarious woe.

I've memories abounding of good times I've shared with you.
And I can tell you here and now that nothing will outdo.
The bond we have of love and trust that
has helped us muddle through.
I speak these words to you today. Every one of them is true.

No tales of bananas, or of broken wooden spoons,
Or getting into trouble when caught reading by the moon.
We won't speak of the time that I set fire to my bed.
Or the time you came to watch me skate,
And heard my potty mouth instead.

I love you, Little Mummy Bear, I can't say it quite enough.
I love that you instilled in me good qualities 'n' stuff.
I'm glad I got to say this now 'cause,
When you're gone it would be tough.
Enjoy this celebration and know,
You got me through the rough.

August 2023

True Love

Kisses every morning and,
Kisses through the day.
Kisses watching television,
And countless other ways.

With gentle touch he reaches out,
To stroke her wrinkled face.
It's really quite romantic how,
They share each other's space.

The love, it is quite genuine.
He's hers and she is his.
I watch them both and know it's true.
There is no greater bliss.

He looks at her as if to say,
You are my only queen,
Then curls up in her lap and purrs.
As his fur he starts to preen.

24/09/2023 12:00

8

Musings

First kiss

My cerebral world came to life yesterday! All the stories, the dreams, the visions ... they're not make believe anymore. The first kiss was so sudden and unexpected, so nervous that we barely knew what happened. That was a shame because I'd have wanted us to remember our first kiss for the rest of our lives. All we will remember now is the shock.

Ah, but the second!

It nearly didn't happen at all. I can see her, even now, sitting there saying "Well, if it's going to happen, you'd better make it now cos I have to go…" all matter of fact like it was the most normal morning of our lives. We must have sat there like that for ten minutes, felt like twenty, was probably only two. I got up and closed the door. That was as much as I could do for another ten minutes. Finally, clumsily, I moved closer. I beckoned her closer – she couldn't. I know she tried because she suddenly turned away saying "I can't do that."

Bringing herself back around to face me, she appeared like a rabbit caught in the glare of oncoming headlights, right before the speeding truck separates it from the life it knew, with an almighty wallop. I recognised this from the feelings coursing through my own body.

Fear, excitement, terror, desire, surprise, and compassion for her plight. Actually, it wasn't quite terror I recognised, though there was something I couldn't read in her eyes. I was on the verge of giving in to my own trepidation, but how could I NOT kiss her now? And yet, I really didn't know if I could, not all premeditated like that.

It had been a split-second moments decision that I wasn't sure I was really doing, until I felt her lips, soft and pliant, on my own. This time it wasn't going to take us both by surprise. I wasn't going to have spontaneity on my side. I could change everything with this next kiss. It could be the biggest mistake I'd ever made. What if she didn't respond, or worse, didn't like it. What if she pulled away at the last moment, unable to go through with it?

What if, when she did respond, I didn't like HER kiss. That's happened before and the awkwardness of it remains. Caution is slapping me about the head with the memory of it. I'm not sure of the exact moment I decided these fears weren't going to paralyse me into inaction, but it came upon me in a rush, and I was suddenly kissing her again.

"Oh lords," I thought, "I did it!" I couldn't read from her kiss anything more than that it was okay that I'd kissed her again. There's one fear conquered.

Suddenly, she kissed me back. Wild, passionate, like there was a fire in her body and her only hope of survival was in this kiss. Her response blew every other fear and doubt from my mind, except the one about how she was going to explain having been here so long.

I reluctantly pulled away, explaining that I'd better let her get home. That was the moment when she turned the tables, shocking ME. Insisting that we'd better share a goodbye kiss to sustain us and pulling me back to her soft mouth. I don't know how long that one little goodbye kiss lasted, neither of us really knows. All I do know is that it was incredible and halted time in its tracks.

All that day, the memory of her kiss lingered on my lips, sweet and gentle with a deep whispering promise. I was already so thankful to her for reawakening my mind and bringing me back to life with our endless conversations on so many topics, long into the night. Little had I known that was merely the first gradual quickening of the night sky before the suns glow brightened the horizon with the promise of dawn. It's all I can do to keep my feet in contact with the ground. They keep wanting to take off and fly!!

Soon

My feet seem perpetually frozen.
The cold gets deep in my bones,
But the sun, it has re-awoken,
Circling closer to hearth and to home.

The snowflakes may catch in my hair,
And the chill wind so eagerly blows,
But it won't be long 'til there's warmth in the air,
And scents of summer will dance in my nose.

23rd June 2012

Awakening

May your dreams bring you warm scented breezes, fresh green meadows, the shade of an ancient oak and dancing sunbeams.

When you tire of all that, feel free to meander down to the stream. The water is cool and almost sweet if you'd like a drink, and if you watch closely the undines can be seen playing in the ripples.

About the author

Gai-Louise (GL to most) resides on the beautiful NSW Central Coast in a modest home that she shares with a stray cat that rocked up to the door one day and declared herself home, an ancient and increasingly grumpy toy poodle with three teeth that he's not afraid to use, and a long-suffering Trak of all trades who provides a huge amount of behind-the-scenes support and has threatened to leave if she brings home anymore strays – human or animal!

Having graced this earth for more years than her mother is equipped to accept, Gai-Louise has accrued some mileage and writes most of her material as a tool for survival, but also finds inspiration in those around her whose qualities she recognises and extols, whilst remaining utterly blind to her own.

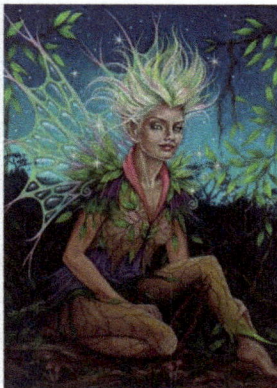

About the artist

Jo Morgan

Jo Morgan portrays the human form in acrylics, watercolour, pastels, and coloured pencil. Her work is included in private collections Australia-wide as well as England, Ireland, Japan, and New Zealand.

Jo Morgan's representations of the human form and human relations have been influenced by her years in the advertising field. Whilst revering men and women her renditions often gently lampoon society's perceptions of the ideal. Her female forms are rarely portrayed in a realistic setting, putting them beyond and sometimes above the ordinary. Jo often takes her inspiration from the images used to advertise.

'We are constantly bombarded with intense images telling stories far beyond the scope of the product they promote. Within these images I find glimpses of emotional intensity not at first obvious and often overlooked within the superficial context of the advertising medium. My 'Intimate Glimpses' series in acrylic is intended to highlight these frozen moments of the human condition, in particular the so-called 'battle of the sexes.'

My art is about beauty but has its feet firmly planted in the soil of sceptical humour. Do we all look like this? No. Should we all look like this? Of course not. But there's no denying we all have a fascination with beauty, we recognise it, and to some degree we all covet it.'

'I've always loved pencils, the feel and smell of them, the satisfaction of a perfectly sharpened point, so indulge myself by working often in colour pencil. It allows a delicacy and control achievable in very few mediums and suits the portrayal of the ethereal wonderfully well. Although I work in other mediums, I always come back to this one for a treat. My exploration of the female form has resulted in several series. These include 'Botanical Beauties' featuring flowers and nudes; the 'Angel' series, probably the most irreverent series portraying less than perfect angels; 'Dreams' series a study of sleep and the magic it performs; the 'Water' series; and the 'Cocktail & Desserts' series, pure fun.'

Born in Sydney in 1956 Jo completed the Commercial Art course at Randwick in 1975 and successfully pursued a career in advertising, working in several major art studios and agencies in Sydney. A move to beautiful Tamborine Mountain in 1985 prompted a change in direction into neon and illuminated displays. Her designs light up casinos and nightclubs throughout Queensland. This background in commercial design and years of rendering client's dreams on paper have provided Jo with a solid grounding in the necessary skills to make the improbable very believable.

'Art is something I have always had to do so I consider myself incredibly lucky to be able to indulge my compulsion and my passion.'

Image credits

	Art by Jo Morgan
Page	**Title**
5	Nuwpi
15	Last Fling
17	A Little Night Mischief
18	Midnight Magnolia
19	What Pedestal?
20	Ocean Treasure
21	Kissed by a Rose
22	Mist Sprite
25	Surrender Without Conquest
26	Naiad's First Breath
27	Essence of Rose
28	The Crimson Slippers
29	Consoling Puff
33	Stolen Moment
35	Sweet Curve
38	Aquavescence
39	Pre-flight Instruction
43	If I Loved You
45	Dance of the Equinaire
46	Hori
53	Sunset Swim
54	All Froth and Bubble
55	Delectable Dish
56	Chocolat
58	Dancing on Fairy Knoll
59	Mating Flight
65	Will You Fly with Me?
71	Wayward Wind *Edited by Gina Potter - September 2023
74	Dreaming
75	The Seedling
76	Waterfall Feys
79	Spring Twilight
81	Flame
83	Releasing the Spectrum

If you love what you've seen here, pop on over to Jo's Redbubble site at https://www.redbubble.com/people/hori/shop and grab yourself something fabulous. There is an impressive range of products to suit every budget. Don't forget to click 'show mature content' (if you're over 18) to see all the images.

Photos	
Cover	"The Road Home" Cellan, Wales, UK – GL Partridge 2015
37	The National 9/11 Memorial & Museum "Men's loafer shoe with tassels. The shoe, completely crushed and covered in dust, was recovered during excavations at Ground Zero sometime between 2006 to 2010." ("25 Heartbreaking Photos Of 9/11 Artifacts - All That's Interesting") - https://allthatsinteresting.com/9-11-artifacts
63	Mum on her honeymoon – Strathavon Manor Guest House, Wyong 1953
64	'Mothers Love' Rose
67	Mum at her 90th birthday wake – Baileys Restaurant and Bar, Tamborine Mtn 2023

Crisis Support Services

Name	Hours	Phone	Website
Emergency	24/7	000	N/A
Beyond Blue	24/7	1300224636	https://www.beyondblue.org.au/
NSW Mental Health Line	24/7	1800011511	https://www.health.nsw.gov.au/mentalhealth/Pages/mental-health-line.aspx
Thirrili NIPS	24/7	1800805801	https://thirrili.com.au/
MensLine	24/7	1300789978	https://mensline.org.au/
QLife	3pm-MN	1800184527	https://www.qlife.org.au/

The above list is far from exhaustive but provides a selection of Australian services. For overseas assistance, please search for local supports in your area.

With very special thanks to:

My incredible support network, including…

Trak –because I am genuinely grateful for all that you do.

Jo – for keeping me on task and for brutally honest feedback.

Marie-Eve and **Emma** – amongst others from CCPC.

Caspa – this work would be <u>nothing</u> without you!

Jo (Lil Big Sis) – I wish you could know how much.

Dr Samuel Farina – the first to explain why it wasn't my fault.

Gina – for awesome on-the-spot editing skills to keep me from the censorship police!

And…

Kemba, HMc, Shyrll and **The Purple Princess of Power** – IYKYK

<u>NOT</u> the end

.

,

Just For You, Dear Reader

Through darkened woods to a warm, blazing hearth,
I thank you for venturing into this maze.
For sharing the journey of my dappled path.
For seeing the beauty hid 'neath the smoke haze.

Upon craggy cliffs in tempest and storm,
You withstood it all as I laid my soul bare.
You walked in the sun and basked in the warm.
My absent companion, I bid you well fare.

Still not the end...

.

;

www.ingramcontent.com/pod-product-compliance
Lightning Source LLC
Chambersburg PA
CBHW070334090426
42733CB00012B/2481